Yesterday's
-No 5-
Wirral
Wallasey, New Brighton & Moreton

ABOVE comic postcard from Moreton — posted in 1917.

COVER Leasowe Lighthouse (see page 23).

PRICE £5.95

By the Same Authors:
Yesterday's Wirral No 1 -   Neston, Parkgate & Heswall
Yesterday's Wirral No 2 -   Birkenhead, Prenton & Oxton
Yesterday's Wirral No 3 -   West Kirby & Hoylake
Yesterday's Wirral No 4 -   Wallasey & New Brighton including Leasowe
Yesterday's Wirral No 6 -   Neston, Parkgate & Heswall including Thurstaston & Irby
Yesterday's Wirral No 7 -   Birkenhead, Oxton & Prenton including Bidston & Upton
Yesterday's Wirral No 8 -   Bebington & Mid Wirral Villages
Birkenhead - A Pictorial History   Birkenhead & surrounding area (Hard back, Published by Phillimore, Chichester)
By the Same Publishers:
The Funny Side of Wirral -   Cartoons by Bill Stott
Another Funny Side of Wirral -   Cartoons by Bill Stott
Liverpool -   Cartoons by Bill Stott
Shadow to Shadow -   History of the Bristol Aeroplane Banwell & BAJ 1941 - 1991
Birkenhead Electric Trams -   Charles Rycroft
The Birkenhead Bus -   T.B. Maund
Murder & Mayhem in Birkenhead - David Malcolm
Railway Stations of Wirral -   Merseyside Railway History Group
The Wallasey Bus -   T.B. Maund

Comic postcard of New Brighton

First Published: 1988
1st Reprint: 1995

Printed by: Eaton Press
                Westfield Road Wallasey Merseyside L44 7JB

Published by: Ian & Marilyn Boumphrey
                "The Nook" Acrefield Road Prenton, Wirral L42 8LD

ISBN 0 9507255 4 4

Introduction

Due to the many excellent photographers who recorded places and events in the Wallasey district from the early part of this century, we are returning to this area. However, as well as Wallasey, New Brighton and Leasowe, which were introduced in our previous publication, we are also featuring Moreton.

Moreton–cum—Lingham (Lingham being the area around Leasowe Lighthouse) had a population of 210 in 1801 rising to 597 by 1901. The name Moreton is said to have meant "the village on the mere" or "the village in the 'Mor', Moor, or tract of wild land." Either of these would be apt as most of the area is below sea-level and was undeveloped up to World War One. Communications to this isolated village were poor until the road from Great Meols to Birkenhead was turnpiked in 1841 and Moreton Railway Station opened on the Wirral Railway Line, 2 July 1866. From the turn of the century Leasowe became a popular camping area in the summer. However, it was not until after the First World War that a housing shortage brought many homeless people to Moreton and by 1921 the population had risen to 4,029. Summer holiday homes became permanent, converted railway carriages, tram cars and shacks occupied the area from the railway line to Leasowe shore. This low-lying area was prone to flooding and the overcrowded housing had no sanitation. It came as no surprise that when the Parish of Moreton became the responsibility of Wallasey Council from April 1928 most of the dwellings were condemned. However, it took ten years to clear the "shanty town" but in the meantime new housing estates had been built and offered alternative accommodation. A fresh optimism had developed and this was further enhanced when Cadburys opened their factory at Moreton in 1953. Today, with the population over 24,000, its new shopping concepts and housing developments are signs that Moreton has shed its old image and entered a new era.

Christ Church Moreton, pictured in Upton Road c. 1908, was built in 1863 to the design of Messrs. Cunningham & Audsley at a cost of £8,000, which included the school (see page 9). The church tower is about one hundred feet high. The cost of building the church and school was met by William Inman of Upton Manor, whose Inman Shipping Line transported passengers and emigrants to America. The building on the left, behind the trees, was the old rectory which stood to the rear of the church near where Chadwick Street now is. It was demolished in 1922.

The number 3 Birkenhead Corporation single-decker bus is standing near Moreton Cross in 1919, the year in which it entered service operating on the Rock Ferry to Moreton route. The driver, dressed in a chauffeur-style uniform, is attending to the front lamp of this "RAF" type Leyland bus which ran from July 1919 until May 1927. The land behind the wall on the left, which is the one seen on the bottom of the opposite page, was known as the Plantation. The pavement on the right is the one in the next picture and the block of houses to the right stands in Upton Road. These buildings were demolished and replaced by a block of shops.

Church Farm, the building on the left, together with its outbuildings behind the wall, stood on the corner of Upton Road and Hoylake Road. Christ Church spire can be seen in the background. The outbuildings in front were demolished in the 1920's. A large sign for the Coach & Horses Hotel (see page 11) stood here in the 1930's. The farm house was demolished and the District Bank built on the site c. 1935. The National Westminster Bank today occupies the building which stands on the corner of Chadwick Street.

This was the view at Moreton Cross c. 1914, taken from Upton Road looking down Station Road (now Pasture Road) with Hoylake Road to the left and the then Birkenhead Road to the right. The building on the left, known as "Carthouse End", became the Manchester & Liverpool District Banking Co., renamed the District Bank in 1924 and was demolished in 1927 (see next page). The shop behind the cyclist was a single storey building and had two steps down to the entrance, which made it prone to flooding. This confectionery shop was then owned by Fanny Birch.

Looking down Hoylake Road towards Moreton Cross c. 1906, the corner of the far end of the whitewashed cottages, can be seen in the previous picture. Moreton Bowling Club building is on the left with the White Horse Whisky sign outside. The sign above "Light Refreshments" tells the traveller that the distances from Moreton were:— Birkenhead 4 miles; Chester 20 miles and London 200 miles. The whitewashed building behind the telegraph pole is the old Coach & Horses Inn which was demolished c. 1927, when the new building was erected. See next picture.

Part of the attractive row of whitewashed cottages seen in the previous picture is shown here twenty years later, shortly before being demolished. The gable-end of the new Coach & Horses is above and to the left of the old one. The old sign board has been removed from above the door which indicates that the licence has been passed from the old building to the new one. This had to be done overnight, otherwise the licence could be lost. This is the reason why new licensed premises were never built on the site of the building they replaced.

Looking up Hoylake Road, the Coach & Horses and the end of the Moreton Bowling Club building beyond, pictured on the right, can be seen on the opposite page. The horse and cart is passing the end of Chapel Lane, now known as Barnston Lane, in this semi-rural scene taken in 1919. The signs inside the entrance to the Bowling Club advise that Tuesdays and Fridays were for members only, and that they served Morris's Wines & Spirits. The licence for the club could have been held by the then landlord of the Coach & Horses, Sylvester Morris.

The photographer must have stood in a similar position, looking up Hoylake Road, to the one who took the previous photograph, but ten years later. The new Coach & Horses, often referred to as the "Cathedral", has replaced the old one which was demolished. The road has been widened and shops have been built. The one behind the two cars, on the corner of Barnston Lane, was a branch of the Birkenhead Co-op Society. The building was previously the Edgerley Cafe and is now a "take-away". A Gateway Supermarket now occupies the site of the old bowling club beyond the Coach & Horses.

HOYLAKE ROAD. MORETON.

This photograph, taken in 1927, is looking down Hoylake Road towards the Cross. The bus in the foreground is a Leyland Leviathan which was in service from May 1927 to June 1933. Immediately to the left of the bus is the old Coach & Horses and towering over it is the new one. The wall and hedge surrounding the new building were demolished at the same time as the old pub, see previous page. The new Lloyds Bank building at the Cross can be seen in the background. The newly built single storey shops on the right were replaced in the 1960's with the present two storey shops.

HOYLAKE ROAD, MORETON.

Rosslyn Drive can be seen to the right of the bus, with Lunt's shop on the corner, taken in January 1929. It was in this month that the Leyland Titan bus pictured came into service for the Wallasey Corporation, operating until December 1936. The Coach & Horses, which can be seen in the background, is featured on the previous pages. The Wrekin, which advertises ices and minerals on the side of its awning, still trades under that name today. The buildings on the left have all been demolished and replaced with shops. The old school house, on the extreme left, can be seen in the next picture.

Moreton Church of England School, Hoylake Road, seen in the previous picture, was opened in 1861 when the population of Moreton-cum-Lingham was 361. The residence for the school teacher, "School House", is seen on the left. By 1927 the population had increased to 15,000 and Cheshire County Council built the Moreton Council School in Upton Road at a cost of £15,000, opening 2 April 1927. Moreton C. of E. School was retained in Hoylake Road as a Primary School until 1973 when it moved into the Upton Road premises, vacated by Moreton Secondary Modern Girls' School. The pictured buildings were closed, then later demolished. The site is now the Village Trader Shopping Centre.

The photographer took this picture standing on the bridge of the Arrowe Brook in Hoylake Road, near its junction with Bermuda Road. The two buses in the photograph at the top of the opposite page are seen here stationary at the terminus. The drivers and conductors are standing by the rear of a Leyland Leviathan bus which has an open staircase. This vehicle entered service with Birkenhead Corporation in 1926. The shops and bungalows on the right, which were built in the 1920's, are still there today. Shops now occupy the site immediately on the left, then Ely Avenue and houses beyond.

Chapel Lane, Moreton, now called Barnston Lane, is pictured here in the early part of this century. The building behind the trees on the left is Old Hall Farm which has a date stone DMW 1719 — probably built for Daniel Wilson, son of Robert Wilson of Bidston Hall, hence the Old Hall name. The building is still there today but used as offices. Yew Tree Farm is seen on the opposite side of the road, sideways on, and was owned by "Bunker" Parkinson. This was demolished in the 1950's and houses were built on the site. The Farmers Arms, which stood behind the wall on the left, is seen in the next picture.

The Farmers Arms is pictured on the corner of Chapel Lane (see previous picture) and Smithy Lane, renamed Netherton Road, in the early part of this century. This pub, which dates back to at least 1860 when William Naylor was landlord, was demolished in 1930 when the present pub was built. The car parking area in front of the present building is the site of the old inn. The smithy stood to the left of the picture but has long since gone and the land now belongs to the brewery. A bomb fell in December 1940, causing a crater further down Netherton Road and two men returning home from the Farmers Arms fell down it!

THE CROSS, MORETON.   No 9.

This 1931 view of Moreton Cross has altered considerably from the one on page 5. Motor transport is becoming more popular, hence the "slow" sign on the road for cars coming from Hoylake Road. The car on the left is at the centre of the cross-roads and the people in the middle of the picture, under the sign post, are waiting for a bus. The shops on the right still have the name plates, between their top windows, of winning horses ridden by the man who built the shops, Titch Mason. He was a local man who rode "Kirkland" to victory in the 1905 National and lived in a house by that name in Pasture Road.

THE CROSS, MORETON,   G.5308.

Taken from a similar position as the previous picture, but five years later in 1936, Moreton Cross is becoming more familiar. The roundabout, which was built in 1935, was considered to be the best way of controlling the traffic at this dangerous junction following several fatal accidents. The sign on the right pointing to the Coach & Horses Hotel, which belonged to the Birkenhead Brewery, advertises "Luncheons, Dinners & Teas." Lloyds Bank is on the left and beyond that is the new Plough Inn which is seen being built in the previous picture with the old building in front. See next page.

This Lacre char-a-banc is standing outside the old Plough Inn in Birkenhead Road (now Hoylake Road), Moreton. Joe Wharton, pictured standing on the right, was landlord of this pub, selling pints and cockles to several generations. It is said there has been an inn on this site since the 1600's, the pictured building being built of local sandstone. In the early part of this century, dances known as the "Fourpenny Hop" were held in a room over the stables, with people walking from as far away as Frankby. This inn was demolished c. 1931 when the present Plough Inn replaced it.

This photograph was taken from the same place as the previous one, but looking away from Moreton Cross, with the wall of the Plough Inn on the left. The building in the centre of the picture, behind the horse and carriage and top hatted man, is still there today with Knutsford Road beyond. "Try Thomas' Bread — Moreton & Upton" is the sign on the back of the horse-drawn bread cart on the right, which is standing outside Brookland House. This farmhouse was demolished and the Sacred Heart Roman Catholic Church built on the site, see picture opposite. The single storey building to the left of the pole is the smithy seen on the next page.

The men on the right are standing in front of the smithy, which once stood in Birkenhead Road (now Hoylake Road) and can be seen in the previous picture. It was well sited on the main turnpike road from Hoylake to Birkenhead which was opened in 1841, and near to the Plough Inn. The building was demolished in the 1950's and Poston Bros. erected a garage on the site, which is now a car spares shop. The single storey, whitewashed building on the left, which was known as Hawthorne Cottage or Wilson's Cottage, had a cottage garden in front. Postons Garage also covered this site.

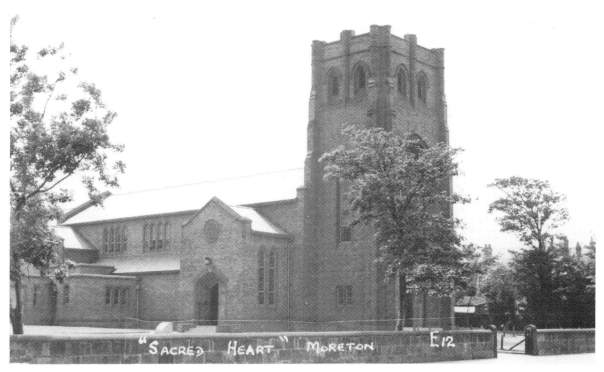

The Sacred Heart Roman Catholic Church is pictured here in Hoylake Road on the corner of Sandbrook Lane. The first services held away from the nearest church of St. Joseph, Upton, were at summer camps by Moreton Shore c. 1900. The first church, in Upton Road, was built at a cost of £1,200 in 1923. Fund raising activity for a new school was held at a field in Sandbrook Lane 20 July 1932. World famous jockeys, including Gordon Richards, rode in donkey races! The new school costing £10,000 opened 20 October 1934. The school hall was used as an overspill church on Sundays to cope with the increased population. The present church opened in 1957.

Looking along Birkenhead Road (now Hoylake Road), away from the Cross, this was the scene in 1909. The row of houses on the left are still there today. Behind the railings on the left was where the Presbyterian Church was built in 1906 at a cost of £800, which also included the cost of the land. The first services were held in the Assembly Rooms, a small wooden structure behind the Plough Inn, on 15 January 1905. Following their success, the foundation stone for the church was laid on 31 January 1906 and was opened by Wm. Lever in June of that year. The building was enlarged in 1937 at a cost of £2,000.

BIRKENHEAD ROAD.

This 1923 view, which is looking away from Moreton towards Birkenhead, was taken in Birkenhead Road. When Wallasey Council took over the Parish of Moreton in April 1928, any duplicated street names were changed and hence Birkenhead Road then became Hoylake Road. The two men who are walking in the direction of Moreton are about to be overtaken by the local police sergeant on his bicycle. Chapel Hill Road is now off to the right, behind the three men. Knutsford Green occupies a site on the left, before the white cottage which can be seen in the next picture.

14

The white house, whose gable end can be seen on the left in the previous picture, is photographed in Birkenhead Road about 1917. This typical country scene with a lady standing outside the thatched cottage and two men in a horse and trap, was taken by E.R. Jones, a photographer from Greasby. This was the main road from Hoylake to Birkenhead, which was built in 1841 and along which many horse-drawn coaches carried passengers. The cottage was demolished between the wars and Chapel Hill Road now occupies the site opposite, to the left of the horse and trap.

Further along Birkenhead Road, away from Moreton, stood the two cottages on the left. Either side of the lady in the horse and trap, topiary chairs can be seen (hedges trimmed to that shape) and on the extreme left, an armchair has been cut out of the hedge. The thatched building was Armchair Farm and the two-storey dwelling was named Old Armchair Cottage. A pub named The Armchair now stands opposite the site of these two cottages which were demolished in 1949. Ennions Farm can be seen in the background on the corner of Reeds Lane.

Poston Brothers' filling station is pictured in Hoylake Road, Moreton c. 1930, near its junction with Stavordale Road (see page 13 for details of their other garage). The three named petrol pumps are from the left: Shell, National Benzole Mixture and Pratts. The garage's breakdown vehicle can be seen on the left and above it is the roof of their motor engineering garage next door, where they repaired and maintained motor vehicles. That building is still there today but the filling station has been replaced with a modern garage.

Longacre Cottage is pictured in Reeds Lane during the early part of this century. As the name suggests, this cottage stood on a long rectangular tract of land, an acre in size. This thatched building was built of local stone with a later brick extension. It had a date stone of 1815 over the door. The wooden box at the front contains bottles of drink which were sold as refreshments to passers-by. In a 1940 directory an Albert Hutty ran refreshment rooms at Longacre but by 1950 this old fashioned dwelling had been demolished and near its site was later built the then Co-op block of shops, at the corner of Birket Avenue.

Station Road, which changed its name to Pasture Road, when Moreton became part of Wallasey in 1928, is photographed prior to 1910. Moreton Cross is seen in the distance between the boys on the right. The two shops with the canopies in front were a newsagent and the nearest one was owned by Job Thomas & Sons, grocers and provisions dealers. A sign on the corner of their shop, in Silverburn Avenue, advises that there was a public telephone installed there. The stone and brick cottages on the left have long since been demolished and the Library now stands behind the site.

This photograph, which was taken in 1914, is also of Station Road, but looking in the other direction from the picture above. The two wooden shacks on the extreme right were demolished and the Moreton Picture House built on the site in 1921 (see next page). Job Thomas & Sons' sign for their grocers shop is above their canopy. The cottages beyond can be seen in the previous picture and behind the trees in the distance stands Ivy Farm. This survived until the 1960's, when Dawson Bros. were the last farmers. It was demolished and the Moreton Youth & Community Centre and Municipal Offices were built on part of the site.

THE CROSS, MORETON.   No 3643

A side view of the Coach & Horses is seen on the right in this 1936 photograph of Pasture Road. Beyond the roundabout and on the right is the newly built District Bank. The shop on the corner of Oakenholt Road, pictured on the left is Irwins, later to become Tesco and now a video shop, with Moreton Picture House on the other corner. Moreton's only cinema opened here 30 April 1921, due to demand following an increase in population from 989 in 1911 to 4,029 in 1921 and also to cater for the holiday-makers at Leasowe. Seating 850, the cinema continued until its closure 28 March 1964 and is a bingo club today.

Taken from Ivy Farm, this photograph looks across Station Road (now Pasture Road), to Mary Anne's Lane, in the early part of this century. The lane was named after Mary Anne's Cottage on the left, which was three cottages in one. The cottage was demolished in 1932, when Pasture Road was widened. The foundation stone of the new Mission Hall was laid 1 May 1932 on a site behind the cottage. The building which had accommodation for 250 is now called Moreton Chapel (Evangelistic) and the narrow roadway is now called Old Maryland Lane.

Moreton Station, which when opened 2 July 1866 on the Hoylake to Birkenhead Line, was primitive, with a cinder platform. It remained a quiet station until the turn of the century when Leasowe became a popular holiday resort and the station was busy in the summer months. This 1923 view shows the platform crowded with Liverpool bound travellers. These include some nuns and a boys' band. This photograph was taken from the bridge which was replaced along with the cinder platform and corrugated iron and timber huts in 1938 when the line was electrified for passenger services. Note the tents in the field on the left which was part of the land on which Cadburys built their factory in 1953. The site was served with its own sidings until c. 1971.

This picture was taken from the same place as the previous one but looking down Pasture Road towards the sea during the First World War. Sunny Side, the row of houses on the left, is still there today. Many of the occupants worked at the Moreton Brick & Tile Company which was to the left of the cottages and whose chimney, which now stands derelict, can be seen in the next photograph. The low-lying land to the right of the fence was built on in 1953 when Cadburys erected their factory. The name has been changed to Premier Brands and the firm is still the largest employer in the area.

Fellowship House, seen in the background behind the group of boys, was initially a boarding house run by Mrs. Eleanor Burden. However, by 1919 when this photograph was taken, holiday homes had been erected in the field in front of the house. As this inexpensive type of holiday became more popular, several of the surrounding fields had chalets built on them (see next picture). The chimney of the Moreton Brick & Tile Company, pictured on the left (see also previous page) is still standing today, unlike Fellowship House which was demolished in the 1950's. Fellowship Garage now stands in front of the site.

Fellowship House, pictured above, expanded its operation under the management of Mrs. Eleanor Burden after the end of the First World War. There was a general housing shortage and Moreton became popular not only as a sea-side resort, but also as a cheap place to live as it was an unrated area. No. 2 Fellowship, a field which had originally provided accommodation for summer holiday homes, is pictured here in 1922 when the dwellings were in permanent use. Being low-lying land, the houses, which had no running water or electricity, were built on stilts or had wheels (see next picture).

This converted vehicle (perhaps a tram car) was the type used as a holiday home in Moreton and then later as a more permanent dwelling. The chalet on the right in the previous picture was originally a railway vehicle but has been transformed by adding steps and a verandah. Although life was difficult, especially in winter when the whole area flooded, there was a tremendous community spirit. There was much resistance when Wallasey Council condemned these properties after becoming responsible for this area in 1928. Some ten years later, by the outbreak of war, about 1,470 dwellings had been removed and the area cleaned up.

The three men in the foreground are sitting on the bridge where the River Birket passes under Pasture Road. St. Tudwal, the house behind the two men on the left, still stands today but many of the others beyond have gone. When this photograph was taken in 1908, Pasture Road extended from Leasowe Common in the distance back to the station, with Station Road then continuing on to Moreton Cross. However, when Wallasey Council took over responsibility for Moreton and Leasowe in 1928, there was already a Station Road in Wallasey, so the full length of the road from Moreton Cross to Leasowe shore was named Pasture Road.

This group who are posing for the photographer after a storm at Moreton in 1919, are ankle deep in water. The man in the foreground is waving a brush in defiance at the weather, whilst others are ready with brushes to clear the site which was at the bottom of Pasture Road on the right at its junction with Leasowe Road. Fred Berry, whose "Grand Stud of Jumpers" merry-go-round is seen in the background, was one of many showmen who visited this site which is still used by visiting fun-fairs and, recently, by a circus.

Taken from Leasowe Embankment in the mid-1930's, this photograph shows how popular this place was. Castle Blake is the house in the distance on the right which still stands on the corner of Pasture Road facing down Leasowe Road. The building with "Refreshments" painted on the roof stood at the junction of Pasture Road and Leasowe Road and was originally a school. Many of the catering huts were still in use when the world's first hovercraft service operated from here to Rhyl between 20 July and 16 September 1962. They have all since been demolished.

The Birkenhead Territorials are on manoeuvres at Leasowe, 11 June 1910. They still relied on horse-power then, as can be seen by at least twenty horses in the picture. Their camp is set up to the left, opposite Leasowe Lighthouse. By 1763 there were two lighthouses at Leasowe, one of them suffered damage and was replaced in 1771, by one on Bidston Hill (not the present building). The one photographed which still stands today bears a 1763 date-stone. There is a view that a new lighthouse was built in 1824. However, there seems to be no contemporary documentary evidence of this. It is probable that the cast-iron staircase was installed in the existing structure at that date.

The flood at Moreton must have come as a surprise, on 25 August 1912, but as the low-lying land was prone to flooding, this intrepid camping family was well prepared. The inside of the tent is raised up on a strong wooden base, upon which stands a kitchen table and chairs and a Primus heater. The barefoot father, with pipe in hand and the air of a ship's captain, surveys the surrounding waterlogged area. His young daughter is perched upon his wife's knee and his older son stands ankle deep in water. The tent is an island which is connected to dry land by the duck-boards father is standing on.

The Liverpool Open Air Hospital for Children was opened 21 July 1914 by Lord Derby. The twelve acre plus site, situated in Leasowe Road opposite Leasowe Castle, was bought 15 July 1900 for £3,300. It was intended to build an isolation hospital for smallpox patients here. However it was for the treatment of tuberculosis that the hospital opened, initially catering for ninety children and increasing to two hundred a year later following a building extension. The beds pictured, which were on wheels, were pushed into the fresh air throughout the year, even in winter! The use of the hospital changed to more general needs in the 1970's. Following closure in the 1980's, it was bought by the Elim Pentecostal Church.

The Leasowe Castle Buffet is pictured on the corner of Reeds Lane and Leasowe Road. This Victorian building which stood diagonally opposite the entrance to Leasowe Castle (see next picture), advertises "Public Refreshment Room" above the main door. It had always been popular as a café, but when it was purchased in March 1932, the new proprietor decided to convert the front part into a general stores, as well as offering teas in the other rooms. The shop would service the new houses being built on the Reeds Lane Estate. The Buffet was demolished and Castle Filling Station built on the site c. 1960.

The Crosville single-decker bus is standing in Reeds Lane, outside Leasowe Castle Buffet (see previous picture) and is facing the entrance to Leasowe Castle. Crosville operated a service from Wallasey to Hoylake via Leasowe and Moreton. To the right of the bus is the gatehouse to the castle and surmounted on stone pillars at the entrance is a pair of stone watch dogs (used as the crest of the Cust family who owned the castle from the 1820's to 1895). The family motto QUI CUST ODIT CAVEAT (he who Cust hates let him beware) is still to be seen carved on the stone pillars.

This rear view of Leasowe Castle was taken in 1934 from a Leasowe Golf Club fairway. The club was formed 12 June 1891 when a course was constructed in the vicinity of Leasowe Lighthouse, which served as a clubhouse. The Lighthouse-Keeper, Mrs. Williams, provided tea and buns for members on Saturday afternoons. In 1893 the club acquired the present ground and additional land was purchased from the trustees of the Railway Convalescent Home after the latter had bought Leasowe Castle in 1910. Some land was lost in 1921 when Wallasey Council bought it under a compulsory purchase order so that Leasowe Road could be widened.

Part of Harrison Drive can be seen in this photograph, taken c. 1912, but most of it is covered in sand. This had been a problem ever since the road to the beach was opened 24 June 1901, especially after a storm. A workman can be seen clearing the pavement and beyond him are three iron drinking fountains which had cast iron drinking cups attached by thick iron chains. The sign on the side of the hut points the way "To the Electric Cars", where the trams could be taken to other parts of Wallasey, see next page. Two rows of wicker chairs, which could be hired from an attendant, can be seen by the waters edge.

THE BEACH AND TENTS, WALLASEY.   No. 3115

This 1931 photograph, taken on the beach near Harrison Drive, shows how people enjoyed themselves then. The rows of tents would be erected for changing in and would also act as a wind barrier. The many flags fluttering in the breeze, must have been a colourful scene. Most of the holiday-makers seem to be overdressed by today's standards and even the paddlers are fully dressed! It was this year that work started on the extension of the promenade from New Brighton to Harrison Drive which included a massive concrete sea wall and promenade 130 feet wide. This was the last section to be completed, opening in 1939.

THE BATHING STATION, WALLASEY.   No 21

The Wallasey Bathing Station, which was established on Wallasey Embankment to the West of Harrison Drive, was opened in 1927. It is pictured here in 1930, when it was described in a local guide as "a sumptuous bathing station with café." It was built for the use of sea-water bathers who could hire costumes and towels here if required. However, its popularity declined after the Derby Baths were built next to the bathing station, to the right of this picture, opening 8 June 1932. The new open-air pool, which cost £35,000, could accommodate 300 bathers and also 200 sun bathers up on the verandah roof. The bathing station was demolished following enemy action during World War Two.

The Grove Hotel, which advertises "Billiards and High-Class Catering", is seen on the corner of Grove Road and Wallasey Village c. 1914. The hotel was built c. 1908 to cater for the visitors who came in their thousands to enjoy the sand and sea at Harrison Drive. Their trade increased dramatically when the last section of Wallasey's tram system, which connected Wallasey Village with the other areas of Wallasey, was opened 7 February 1911. The number 62 tram on the left operated from 1913 until 1933, the letter "P" denoting the Poulton route. The Grove Hotel building was burnt down in the 1960's and demolished.

Two keen golfers are playing at the Wallasey Municipal Golf Course in 1913. The wooden club house and professional's shop can be seen behind the players, with Sea Road beyond. The house on the extreme left is now No. 25 Warren Drive on the corner of Linksway. Originally New Brighton Golf Club, which was founded in 1890, boasted its own railway station, Warren Halt. This stood at the bottom of Sea Road on the east side but became disused and was closed 1 October 1915. The nine hole golf links was bought by the Council in 1910 for £15,500. (See next picture).

Warren Golf Club was founded on the links here in 1911 and is believed to be the oldest golf club playing over a municipal course. This large house, Wallasey Grange, and its grounds were purchased in 1923 by the Council for £7,000. Opening 2 April 1924, it became the golf clubhouse, housing the professional's shop and also a café. The old wooden buildings, pictured above, were demolished, the site later becoming the old ninth green. Wallasey Grange was built in 1862 for a Major Walter, who was a Liverpool shipowner, and prior to 1923 had housed the Wallasey Grange School.

St. George's Road, which was originally known as Back Lane, is pictured c. 1908, when it was a narrow private road. As with other roads in the area the coming of the tram system to Wallasey Village in 1911 meant dramatic change. It was the Wallasey Tramways and Improvements Bill of 1909 that gave the go-ahead for the final stretch of track on the Wallasey system that altered this peaceful scene. The track ran from Wheatland Lane via St. Lukes Church; Mill Lane; Marlowe Road; Wallasey Road; Claremount Road; Broadway; St. George's Road; Sandy Lane and Wallasey Village to Grove Road. The building on the right, which was cut back to the second chimney, is now Braddafield, No. 32, St. George's Road.

Taken in 1907 from beyond Folly Lane on the right, this picture looks across to St. George's Road School. In 1864, Wallasey Grammar School moved from its building in Breck Road, which still stands today, to premises in Back Lane (now St. George's Road) and in 1876 moved again to Withens Lane. Wallasey National School took over the vacated building to accommodate boys. In 1907 the buildings were rebuilt to include girls and infants from School Lane (see page 35) and today are known as St. George's Primary School. The houses on the left are in Perrin Road and the site in front of the houses is now occupied by Wallasey Village Library.

The children in the distance are walking down the paved part of Folly Lane. This cobbled path led from Claremount Road at the top to Wallasey Village at the bottom. This rural scene, taken in 1906, with its overhanging trees on the right and brambles on the left, was to change dramatically with the coming of the tram system to Wallasey Village in 1911. The wall leading up the hill on the right borders the grounds of the house, Hilary Breck. This wall is pictured behind the tram below but has been rebuilt. The vertical wall on the extreme right is the side of the cottage, also in the next picture.

When the tram system was extended to Wallasey Village, opening 7 February 1911, many old lanes, like Folly Lane pictured above, were altered and their character gone forever. The cottages on the right, whose corner can be seen in the picture above, were demolished by 1913 when the wall surrounding the Parish Church was extended to enclose the site. The No. 46 tram can be seen negotiating the newly built road called Broadway. This steep gradient had a speed limit of 4 mph descending and 8 mph ascending; all trams on this route were fitted with slipper brakes.

Although this rural view of Claremount Road, taken in 1910, has changed somewhat, the building on the right is today numbered 44 and 46 and the building beyond, on the corner of Prospect Vale, is No. 48. Behind the telegraph pole stands Wallasey Cottage Hospital which was built in 1885. The hospital closed 8 August 1980 and Nightingale Lodge, offering sheltered accommodation, was built on the site. Clare Lodge, which stood on the left behind the lamp post, was built by Rev. Clayton Green when he retired from running Claremount School. The school, which stood near Lyndhurst Road, had been named after Clare College, Oxford, where he graduated.

The funeral cortège of Frederick Krueger is seen proceeding towards the Parish church 13 March 1909. He lived in loneliness and died in squalor, yet when he died Wallasey villagers clubbed together so he would not be buried in a pauper's grave. He came to Wallasey c. 1878 as a stranger, living in various makeshift dwellings for 10 years then settling in a corrugated iron hut off Green Lane. His family had been on the personal staff of the Emperor of Prussia and following a university education he practised law and was also a concert pianist as well as a composer. The secret of why he gave all this up to live a secluded life in Wallasey died with him.

Willow Cottage, with a date-stone R-IOM-1737, was run as Willow Nurseries at 134, Wallasey Village in this 1930's photograph. To the right of the lamp post, between the pedestrians, was a path called Big Yard which led through to St. George's Road. Beyond the path was Pear Tree Farm, named after a big pear tree which stood in front of the farm. The next building, which juts out, number 144, was a "reliable boot repairer" and at Nos. 150 to 154 was Chas. Dalrymple's upholsterers shop. Then followed a row of three terraced cottages and at No. 162 was the Traveller's Rest (see picture below).

The Traveller's Rest, pictured in the 1930's, is the distant building in the picture above. This old, sandstone, beer-house had two small rooms; the bar parlour and the news room. This was one of the properties that had been ear-marked in the widening and straightening scheme, prepared by the Corporation as far back as 1906. The Traveller's Rest had closed down by the outbreak of war in 1939, by which time half the property had been acquired by the Corporation. The go-ahead for demolition of the war-damaged or derelict property was given in 1946. The site of all the buildings pictured above is occupied by St. Mary's College, which opened in 1973.

In this photograph taken about 1909, the lamp post with horse trough beneath stands at the top of Leasowe Road at its junction with Wallasey Village. The single-storey building to the left of the trough was opened 7 January 1889 as reading rooms which later became the library. It was demolished in the 1960's when the road was widened and the new block of shops set further back. The tall building in the background is still numbered 139 and 141 on the corner of Beechwood Avenue. Hamilton Bros. bread shop is seen behind the girl on the extreme right. These premises still stand on the corner of St. John's Road and are now an estate agent's office.

Taken from the top of Leasowe Road in 1913, the two gates in the wall on the right led to numbers 2 and 4. It was in 1921 that it was proposed to widen Leasowe Road. The total cost of the three mile length of Leasowe Road and Reeds Lane was to be £135,000 split ⅔ to Wirral Council and ⅓ to Wallasey Corporation after the Ministry of Transport had provided 50% of the cost. One of the victims of the scheme was to be Spragg's Vale Brewery buildings, pictured on the left between the trees. The brewery, which was established c. 1840, had 5 licensed houses by 1910, of which two were fully licensed. They were taken over by Higsons in 1920.

These old cottages are pictured in Wallasey Village prior to the First World War. The old Cheshire Cheese stood on the site of the pavement and roadway on the right. The front of the building was level with the other cottages. It was demolished in 1885 and the present Inn set back and the road widened. The white building at the end of the row of cottages was the Swiss Laundry Company and the shop jutting out at the end was Mrs. Campbell's sweet shop on the corner of Folly Lane. The premises on the right had all been demolished by 1932 and those on the left by 1950.

These two thatched cottages are photographed in School Lane in 1905. Sam's Cottage on the right, named after Sam Salisbury, was gable-end on to the lane and the last example of the very old wooden cruck principle. The cottages were long, low, with a straw thatch and sometimes had an upper room, as in this case. A cruck was the name given to the tree trunks or large boughs leaning against each other to form the skeleton of the building. Sam's Cottage received a direct hit from a bomb in March 1941 and was completely destroyed. Carlyle's Cottage on the left survived the war but was demolished when School Lane was widened.

St. Hilary's Girls and Infants School began in 1840 and was initially housed in the home of the sexton, Mr. A. Coventry. In 1847 the school-house pictured was erected in the narrow lane seen in the previous picture which was hence named School Lane, having previously been called The Gutter. Miss Railton became the school mistress in 1859. The school continued to educate the young girls of the village until 1907, by which time the population had increased to such an extent that a new boys' and girls' school was built in St. George's Road and the girls moved from this old building which was then sold.

St. Hilary's Girls School, seen in the previous picture was sold for £600 in 1907 to Penrose James. This building could have been used as the parish hall but was too far away from the church. Instead the proceeds from the sale went towards paying for the new parish hall in Wallasey Village, costing a total of £2,870, which opened 13 December 1906. The former school-house was rented to J. M. Evans & Company, buildings and contractors, but by 1914 they had moved to new premises at 131 Wallasey Village. The building was then used as a smithy by Harry Morgan. A hoist was rigged up, an upstairs window knocked out, the aperture widened.

Taken from Bidston footpath in 1910, this photograph looks up at St. Hilary's, Wallasey's Parish Church, which was built in 1859 and whose separate Tudor tower dates back to 1530. The houses on the right are now numbers 1 and 3 St. Hilary Drive and on the extreme right is Wyncliffe, 6 St. Hilary Drive. Below and to the right of the tower can be seen the old girls' school which is being used by a building contractor (see previous page). The row of buildings to the right, facing the open field, is numbers 1 — 17, Beaufort Drive. Mosslands School which stands in Mosslands Drive now occupies the site in the foreground.

This odd-looking building, pictured in 1912, stood at the bottom of St. Hilary's Brow at its junction with Breck Road. Between the gap in the walls on the right a path led up to the old Wallasey Windmill which stood on the Breck from 1765 until it was demolished in 1887. A house called Millthwaite was built on the site of the Mill, which was subsequently replaced by Millthwaite Court Flats. A directory of 1915 describes the resident of 2 St. Hilary's Brow as Miss Christine Merriman — Tobacconist, and the same building was also listed under Hillside, Breck Road. The building was demolished about 1930 when St. Hilary's Brow was widened. The site now forms part of the widened road.

This photograph taken from Breck Road c. 1908 shows the Pool Inn, in the centre, on the corner of Poulton Road. In about 1880 this Inn replaced the original seventeenth century building which stood below the present one in Poulton Bridge Road off to the right. The horse-drawn omnibus, which originally plied the streets of London, bore the lettering "Seacombe, Poulton and Wallasey Omnibus Company — Seacombe Ferry & Poulton." Although this company was never formed under that name, it did operate between the two destinations from 1907 until the tram service started a similar route in July 1910. The water trough beneath the lamp post was ample reward for the thirsty horses.

The large stone in front of the wall on the right is in Mill Lane, on the corner of Poulton Road. It can be seen in the picture above, to the right of the horse, with children playing on it. Mrs. Torrence's shop on the left, in Poulton Bridge Road, was described in a 1915 directory as "Poulton Town Sub-P.O. & M.O. Office. Mrs Mary Torrence — also grocer and provision dealer." It was not a Sub-Post Office for very long, but remained a grocers shop and then a newsagents until the building was demolished in the 1960's, when the road was widened and made into a dual carriageway. Poulton Victoria Sports & Social Club is now on the site behind the shop.

A photographer was on hand to record this fire at number 154 Victoria Road, Seacombe 29 May 1906. The gathered crowd are looking up at the shopkeeper's wife, Mrs Sandeman, being rescued from the smoke-filled window via a window cleaner's ladder. Two men ran to the Seacombe Fire Station in Brougham Road, which was unmanned, got the horse from the stable, mounted the carriage and drove to the fire. This quick-thinking action saved the premises and adjoining shops from burning down. Devine Bros. grocery store, which can be seen on the corner of Florence Road, is still standing today, but the next three buildings have all been demolished, with the Seacombe Conservative Club now occupying the end one.

This advertising post card for the Irving Theatre, Victoria Road, Seacombe (now Borough Road), was used by Mr. James Kiernan, the proprietor and manager, in 1908. It was he who built the theatre, naming it after the famous actor Sir Henry Irving who opened it 18 December 1899. An early poster advertised "opera, burlesque, pantomime and drama" for this 900 seat theatre. Following a fire in 1908 and after extensive renovations, it became the King's Theatre. Changing its name several times, it became the Embassy Cinema in 1936, although films had been featured on and off since 1904. The last film was shown 21 March 1959 and the building is now a bingo hall.

The North & South Wales Bank, Seacombe Branch, is in the centre of this 1905 picture, the stone crest of the Prince of Wales' Feathers can still be seen on top of the building. The bank was taken over by the Midland but that closed and the building is now a bistro named La Banque. Victoria Road (now Borough Road) is straight ahead and Brighton Street off to the right. Burrow's Champion Boot Stores, pictured on the right, can also be seen in the photograph below to the left of the lamp post, under which a policeman stands in this view.

The photographer was standing in the middle of Victoria Road, pictured above, and was looking towards the lamp post in the centre. Brighton Street is off to the left with the property on the corner, containing the Central Grocery Shop and Burrow's Boot Stores, being known as Cambrian Buildings. The clock building on the corner of Church Road displays advertising for Entwistle Bros. Ltd., Artificial Teeth Manufacturers. The Five Bars Rest, a public house, now occupies the building. The part of Victoria Road, which continues behind the lamp post is now Borough Way, a cul-de-sac with pedestrian access beyond.

King George V and Queen Mary visited Wirral 25 March 1914. Their first engagement was luncheon on a train in a Hooton siding. Their itinerary then included a visit to Lever Bros., Port Sunlight; Cammel Laird's Shipbuilding Yard in Birkenhead; Town Hall, Birkenhead where the King pressed an electric button to open an extension of the Bidston Hill recreation area; then via Poulton Bridge and Mill Lane to Central Park, Liscard, where the stand pictured had been erected. It was from here that the King pressed another button to lay the foundation stone for Wallasey Town Hall. The Royal carriage is receiving a farewell wave from the Mayor, Ald. T. V. Burrows, as it sets off for Seacombe Ferry, see below.

The Royal carriage, having set off from Central Park, Liscard (see picture above), proceeded to Seacombe Ferry via Church Street, Brighton Street, Church Road and Victoria Place. This was the scene in Brighton Street, which was typical of the welcome awaiting the King and Queen, with bunting draped over every building. Edwin Palmer's fancy drapers shop, which is behind the lamp post on the right, has been well decorated. The large T.P. sign, on the end of the next block of buildings, is on the side of Tom Pagon Clugston's confectioners shop, on the corner of Harrowby Road.

The horse in front of the milk-cart appears to have six legs. The two extra ones actually belong to a child who is behind the vehicle. The cart is outside numbers 29 and 31 Church Street, Egremont c. 1915. The road to the right of the tram is Church Avenue, and the former Town Hall near the junction with Brighton Street, is the domed building above the tram. This building was taken over by the education committee and used as a technical school when the new Town Hall was opened in 1920 (see below). All the buildings pictured were destroyed during Wallasey's worst air raids of the Second World War, 12 — 14 March 1941. In the 1960's, flats were erected on the right and are currently being refurbished.

Wallasey Town Hall is pictured from the promenade overlooking the Mersey in 1920. It was in 1900 that talks started on the site for the new Town Hall which was to replace the one in Church Street (see picture above). There were several years of discussion which became known as the "Battle of the Sites." The Brighton Street plan won the day, the contract being given to Moss & Sons of Loughborough. The foundation stone was laid by King George V 25 March 1914. However, the war intervened and the building was opened 12 August 1916 as a military hospital. Over three hundred beds were in use, treating some 3,500 wounded men during the war. The Town Hall was officially opened 3 November 1920.

The Lancashire Navy League National Sea Training Home for Boys was situated in Withens Lane, next to Wallasey Grammar School. The foundation stone was laid on the Clifton Hall Estate, overlooking the Mersey, 18 October 1902 and the home opened 2 October 1903. The Navy League was established to admit poor boys desirous of going to sea. They were educated, fed, clothed and trained in the practical duties of seamen, found berths on ships and given a free rig-out. The boys are posing here with their training officers in 1905. The building was evacuated during World War II and eventually opened as Wallasey Technical College in 1949.

The foundation stone for St. Mary's Parish Church, pictured on the corner of Withens Lane and Manor Lane, was laid 13 January 1877 and the church consecrated 13 December. The congregation first met in a Mission House situated in Liscard Village which was licensed for divine service in 1870. The new Parish, which was formed in 1877, extended from Liscard Village to the promenade and from Martins Lane to Earlston Road. Mrs Mary Anne Maddock, who lived at Liscard Manor (now Earlston Library), donated the land upon which the Church and Parish Hall, which opened in 1898, were built. The square tower was erected in 1882.

LISCARD ROAD, WALLASEY.   W.S.10.

Liscard Road is pictured here in the late 1930's with Seacombe Presbyterian Church on the right at the corner of Brougham Road. The site was originally occupied by Brougham House which was also known as Frog Hall, possibly due to a pond which once lay in front of it. The church purchased Brougham House for £1,550 in 1906 but due to lack of funds the foundation stone was not laid until 29 July 1911 and the church opened 25 September 1912. It had moved from its previous premises in Church Road, Seacombe which had opened in 1869, the Church having been founded in 1862. The shop beyond is on the corner of Hood Street and still trades today as a pet shop.

St. Johns Church, Liscard.

The square Grecian design church is St. John's and stands in Liscard Road. The land which once belonged to Birkenhead Priory was part of that purchased by Sir John Tobin from F. R. Price c. 1830. The church, which opened 19 May 1833, could accommodate up to 1,500 worshippers. A complete renovation and redecoration was carried out in the centenary year of 1933 at a cost of £700. The church suffered damage during the Second World War which was not fully repaired until 1954. The number 33 tram in this 1914 photograph was built in 1905 by United Electric Car Company Limited of Preston. The bowler-hatted gentleman is sitting next to the W.D. sign, which meant the tram operated on the Warren Drive route.

Liscard Village looked like this in 1913 with the tram in the foreground, number 50 on the Warren Drive route, heading down Liscard Road. The pagoda-like building erected in 1904 was a passenger shelter and popular meeting place known as the Monkey House. The poster to the left of the shelter is seen attached to railings which protected steps leading down to men's toilets. The Monkey House was demolished in 1926 and was later replaced by a roundabout since changed to the one-way traffic system completed in 1979. Williams' Bros. grocers shop is on the left and the next building was opened 22 August 1908 as the Bank of Liverpool and is now Barclays Bank.

There has been a Wellington Hotel on the corner of Wallasey Road and Sea View Road, Liscard, since at least 1850 when the landlord was William Bird, who in 1860 was described as a car proprietor. To supplement his income, he probably operated a horse and cab service linking Liscard with the ferries to Liverpool, and with Birkenhead via Poulton Bridge. A plot next to the Wellington Hotel on the Seaview Road side was purchased as the site for a replacement, the foundations of which were laid in June 1936. The new hotel, seen behind the advertising hoardings, was opened in 1937. The old pub was demolished and the site is now part of Wallasey Road.

The Boot Inn in Wallasey Road, is pictured c. 1903 soon after it had been altered from a quaint irregular building, which had a large water butt placed in a recess in front. This hostelry dated back to Elizabethan times and was reputed to have been named after a boot containing gold which had been rescued from a robber by the landlord and returned to its rightful owner. The original boot, which had been left as a sign for the inn, is said to be the one preserved in the present Boot Inn, together with the full legend. The inn pictured was demolished in 1925 and the present one which replaced it was built on a site to the rear.

The Mill Lane Infectious Diseases Hospital was opened September 1887 in an 8 bed pavilion with a small administrative block and a hand laundry. The hospital was extended in 1894 and in 1901. The terms here in 1904 were from five shillings (25p) to two guineas (£2.10) per week, but any person unable to pay was also admitted. By 1925, the hospital site had more than doubled to just under 7 acres with an extensive range of buildings which could treat 66 patients. In 1921 a large house in Mill Lane called Highfield was purchased by the Council and became the first Maternity Hospital in the area. The building pictured is now the unit headquarters for nursing administration.

This semi-rural picture taken c. 1911 in Mill Lane, Liscard, shows a horse and cart beyond the old man with a wheelbarrow. The spire of St. Alban's Church can be seen on the left. Built in the Gothic style at a cost of £2,500, it was the first Roman Catholic Church constructed in the area, opening 18 September 1853, at the junction of Mill Lane and St. Alban's Road. Behind the railings, to the left of the four shops, stood Liscard Water Tower which was built in 1861 as a distribution centre for water. It is now a listed building and houses a tyre depot. The white-washed cottage on the right can be seen below.

This white-washed cottage, surrounded by trees, once stood in Mill Lane, at what is now the junction of Dinmore Road, and can be seen in the picture above. The thatcher, who is working on the roof, was probably not a local man, as the nearest one in a directory of the period, was at Knutsford. It was known as Keenan's Cottage, being named after Harry Keenan, who was caretaker of the water tower opposite, which was also used by the fire brigade. When the fire alarm was raised, the key was obtained from Harry Keenan and a pull-cord sounded the bell at the top of the tower. Upon hearing this, the volunteer firemen rushed to the tower and dragged the hose-reel out (see next picture).

The firemen referred to previously were organised on a voluntary basis under a Captain Leather. The Wallasey Fire Engine Station was situated next to the water tower in Mill Lane, but in the 1890's had moved to a site at the junction of Manor Road and Liscard Village. A full-time superintendent was appointed and a steam fire engine bought. In 1900, a chemical engine was acquired and used until 1914. It was this year that the Central Fire Station pictured, was built on land adjacent to the existing station, opening 23 October 1915. The station was moved to its present site in Mill Lane in 1986 and the buildings were demolished, the site becoming a car park.

COTTAGES, LISCARD VILLAGE. P&CºLºL

The long, low cottage behind the gate, pictured about 1907, stood opposite Liscard General Post Office. Split into two dwellings, the larger thatched part was in Liscard Village and the smaller part with a tiled roof had its entrance in Egerton Grove, opposite the houses pictured in the background. This type of dwelling was known as a cruck cottage, after the tree trunks or boughs which leant against each other to create the arch design of the building. Cross-pieces joined them together to form a capital A shape and these were connected by ridge-pieces to create a skeleton. The sides being filled with cob (straw and clay) or rough masonry and with a thatched roof. Demolished c. 1924, Hebron Hall was then built on the site.

The driver and conductor of the No. 13 Wallasey tram pose for the photographer at the Seaview Road Depot c. 1908. Both electric tram and depot came into operation 17 March 1902. This was one of 25 four-wheel, double deck, open top Wallasey trams built in 1902 by the Electric Railway & Tramway Carriage Works Ltd., of Preston. By mid 1905, all the original trams had been fitted with Bellamy tops as pictured. An extension to the depot in 1907, which incorporated the brick arch to the left, meant that 68 cars could be accommodated here. When the trams ceased here in 1933, buses occupied the garage until the depot closed 26 October 1986, transferring to Laird Street, Birkenhead. The site is now being developed as a superstore.

Edward VII visited Liverpool to lay the foundation stone for the new Anglican Cathedral 19 July 1904 and having previously proclaimed it an official holiday, some 8,000 people attended the service. Although the King and Queen did not set foot on Wirral soil, onlookers from this side of the river could see the royal couple leave the Mersey in the Royal Yacht "Victoria & Albert." This visit was used as an excuse by Wallasey Corporation to illuminate and bedeck the tram. A bust of King Edward is positioned above the driver, who can be seen between the bunting. This photograph was one of many taken by Moorhouse, Photographer, Egremont and published as a postcard.

FREE LIBRARY, LISCARD.   J. C. Smith, Post Office, Liscard.

The Wallasey Free Public Libraries were instituted in 1898 and a rate of one penny in the pound imposed. The Central Library was located in Earlston House, which had been acquired by the Council in 1898, opening 24 March 1900, with the reference section opening 25 January 1902. This library proved very popular, with 227,789 books being lent in the first two years. Following a gift of £9,000 from Mr. Andrew Carnegie, a new Central Library was erected adjoining the old building, opening 30 September 1911. Part of the old library was destroyed during the Second World War, the site is now the staff car park.

The Telegraph Inn was built in 1841, the same year as new stations were built on the Holyhead to Liverpool telegraph line. The Telegraph is situated on one of the highest points in Wallasey and a favourite theory as to the choice of name is that it commanded good views, not only over Liverpool Bay and the River Mersey, but also across to the telegraph station on Bidston Hill. The history of the Telegraph is no doubt also connected with the old powder magazines, only a few minutes away, supplying ships waiting at anchor with stores and beer. At the turn of the century the grocery business was given up, turning the Telegraph into a simple ale-house. A spirit licence was not applied for until 1964.

Picture by Bob Hughes

Emmanuel Church can be seen on the left in this 1920's photograph of Seabank Road. An iron mission chapel stood on this site in 1879 and was replaced when the eastern portion of the pictured church was consecrated in 1900. This area was part of St. Jame's Parish until 1909, when the church was completed, then forming a separate parish. The number 70 tram, travelling towards Egremont, was one of the last batch of ten trams ordered by Wallasey Corporation in 1920. Magazine Lane is on the extreme left, with the shops, which are still there today, numbering 156 to 170, the third from left being pictured below.

Albert Ernest W. Howard's shop was situated at 166 Seabank Road, New Brighton (see picture above). Probably taken prior to World War I, Albert Howard and family pose for a photograph in front of his shop which has been meticulously decorated with poultry and game. Braces of pheasant hang from the top rail, turkeys and chicken below them, and duck and geese are arranged on the table. This type of display may seem unhygienic and ostentatious today, but was normal practice then. The salesman on the left wearing the beret is oblivious of the photographer and is conducting a sale with a customer.

This view, with New Brighton Tower standing proudly in the background, was taken on Magazine Brow c. 1904. The steps in the wall on the left are still there today but the trees behind have all been cut down. Fort Cottage, which is to the left of the pedestrian has a datestone of 1841. Beyond that is Eve's Cottage which is reputed to be over 200 years old and was named after the author's aunt, who lived there in the 1950's. Behind the high wall on the right was Liscard Battery, the chimneys belonged to the buildings in the next picture. Houses numbering 28 to 38 were built on the site. The castellated gateway at the end of the wall is still there today.

The courtyard of the Liverpool Yacht Club is pictured here during the First World War. The Mayor, in the centre of the photograph, is surrounded by soldiers, many of whom are wounded. In October 1912 the Yacht Club purchased the former Liscard Battery, which had become obsolete, for £1,620. The battery was built in 1858, armed with guns and provided accommodation for regular soldiers. The inside of the entrance gates which are still there today, can be seen in the background, directly above the Mayor. Liscard Magazines, where ships deposited their gunpowder during their stay in Liverpool, had been sited near the Battery on the other side of Fort Street, from c. 1768 until 1851, when vessels anchored off New Ferry were used.

WAR MEMORIAL. NEW BRIGHTON

The War Memorial pictured on Magazine Promenade was erected using funds raised by public subscription. It was sculptured by Birnie Rhind of Edinburgh and was unveiled by Lord Derby on 26 January 1921, in memory of 848 men of the borough who died in the 1914-18 war. A further inscription was added at the end of the Second World War. The castellated towers on the right, which still stand today, guarded the entrance to the Liscard Battery. The buildings to the right of the memorial can be seen in the previous picture and some of the buildings on the left are being demolished. The rear gardens of 28 to 38 Magazine Brow now occupy this site.

No book about New Brighton would be complete without a mention of Mother Redcap's. Famous in the eighteenth and early nineteenth centuries as an ale house, the original building erected c. 1595 was rebuilt in 1888 and the Victorian building was later used as a cafe. It stood between the present Lincoln Drive and Caithness Drive and was originally the only dwelling between what are now Seacombe and New Brighton. Mother Redcap, who gave the inn its name, was said to be the custodian of many seafarers' treasures. When she died, however, very little property was found and could still be hidden there today! The building was demolished in 1974 and the site remains empty. A comprehensive account of Mother Redcap's can be found in "The Rise and Progress of Wallasey."

New Brighton Water Tower in Gorsehill Road, the highest point in Wallasey, is still a landmark on the skyline today as it was when opened 83 years ago. The first reservoir was brought into use in 1887, followed by the second which opened at the same time as the water tower, in February 1905. These two covered reservoirs are situated to the left of the water tower and have a capacity of over six million gallons. They are fed by local well-water at Liscard and also by a supply from Lake Vyrnwy in North Wales. The reservoirs were damaged by a high explosive bomb in May 1941 and were not fully repaired until 1948. New Brighton Tower can be seen behind the houses.

38119   VICTORIA ROAD, NEW BRIGHTON   VALENTINES SERIES

Many photographs taken during the first twenty years of this century in New Brighton included New Brighton Tower in the background. This one, taken in Victoria Road c. 1904, shows the tower, as did the picture above. The number 18 open-top tram, which has just turned into Victoria Road from Rowson Street, was one of the first consignment of twenty-five taken into service in 1902. It was fitted with a "Bellamy" short top cover in 1904. This increased its earning capacity in bad weather. The building behind the horse-drawn cart which was then John Kellitt & Sons grocers shop, has since been demolished and the site is now an open space.

SEACOMBE FERRY.

0694

Horse-drawn and motorised vehicles can be seen on the deck of the luggage boat "Seacombe", pictured at Seacombe Ferry during World War I. She was built by Cochran & Company of Annan and started in service in 1901 plying the Mersey to Liverpool until 1921. The "Leasowe" and "Liscard" took over, followed in 1929 by "Perch Rock". Although the Mersey Tunnel, which was opened in 1934, took most of the vehicular trade, it was not until March 1947 that the steamer service ceased. The floating landing-stage pictured, which was built in 1880, was replaced by one providing a berth for passengers, a berth for vehicular traffic, and one for either. It was opened by Lord Derby 23 October 1926.

Taken on the approach to Seacombe Ferry c. 1931, the nearest tram is number 68 bound for Warren Drive. This was one of six trams in the Wallasey fleet built in 1915 by the Brush Electrical Engineering Company Limited and had the honour of being Wallasey's last tram on 1 December 1933. The tram behind with the letter P on the lower window, which meant it ran on the Poulton Road Route, is number 69. This was one of the last batch of ten trams ordered, which was delivered in 1920 and it was withdrawn from service in February 1933. The number 6 bus to the left is a Leyland Titan TD1 which operated from January 1929 to December 1936.

Seacombe Promenade, which is pictured here in 1906, was the third stage of linking Seacombe and New Brighton by continuous promenade. The initial construction from the bottom of Sandon Road to Egremont Ferry commenced in 1891 and in 1899 was continued to beyond New Brighton Pier. This portion between Seacombe and Sandon Road was commenced in 1901. The block of four houses pictured on top of the left bank was called River View. Access was via the part of Demesne Street which is now called River View Road. The site was bought by the council in 1905 and the buildings demolished. Guinea Gap Baths were built there opening in 1908 (see picture below).

Guinea Gap Baths, which were built on the site of the buildings pictured above, were opened 7 April 1908 by Mr. T. V. Burrows, Chairman of the Health Committee. These were the first municipal baths for Wallasey and were built at a cost of £15,000, using sea-water pumped from the Mersey. Prior to the promenade being built in 1901, there was a breach in the river bank here known as Guinea Gap. This was a popular place for swimming as it was free from dangerous currents. It was off here that the Seacombe and Egremont Swimming Club, founded in 1890, held meetings and competitions. It moved to the new baths at Guinea Gap in 1908 and changed its name to the Wallasey Swimming Club in 1913.

The Egremont Ferry pictured here c. 1904 was the one designed and built 1874-76 by the Manager, William Carson. The original ferry had been built c. 1828 by Captain Askew. The iron pier and run-out stage, which ran on rails, were joined by a link stage, which can be seen attached to two tripods, connected by an arch and straddling the pier. This enabled boats to land even at low tide. However, when the tide was out, as seen here, the link stage was very steep for passengers. The children in the foreground are standing on the grid iron, which was used to clean and repair ferry boats at low tide. The landing stage was replaced in 1909, see picture below.

EGREMONT PIER

This 1917 view of Egremont Pier, as altered in 1909 (see picture above) shows that the iron tripods have gone; the pier extended and the floating landing stage at right angles to the pier. The buildings fronting the stage, including the engine house for working the run-out stage, have been demolished and a shelter built on the site. The ferry was re-opened 8 November 1909 by Mr. John Joyce, the Chairman of the Ferries Committee. This floating stage operated until 1929 when it had become unsafe and was replaced with a larger one, which was moored by anchors and chains, the old pier being retained. The next event in the ferry's history occured in 1932 (see next picture).

The floating landing stage at Egremont Pier is literally floating away in this 1932 photograph. The landing stage, which had been replaced in 1929 (see previous picture) was rammed by a large oil tanker, the "British Commander", 21 May 1932. The 75 ton bridge was lifted the same day by the "Mammoth" floating crane to West Float Dock, Birkenhead. The repair cost was £7,340 and the ferry was back in service by 1933. The final blow came 12/13 May 1941, when the coasting steamer "Newlands" collided with the end of the pier and the ferry was finally closed for good. The work of demolishing the stage and pier was completed by August 1946.

This Edwardian view, with the ladies wearing long dresses and ornate hats, was taken on the promenade deck of the "Lily" in the summer of 1905. The "Rose" and her sister ship the "Lily" were built for Wallasey Ferries by John Jones & Son of Liverpool in 1900/1, each having accommodation for 1,831 passengers. These twin screw steamers were the prototypes for the passenger boats that followed and finally ended the paddle-steamer era. They served the Wallasey Ferries well, operating mainly on the Seacombe to Liverpool service until 1927, when they were succeeded by the "Marlowe" and "Wallasey". They both became passenger tenders at Queenstown, Ireland. Crowds of people can be seen behind the boat at Pier Head, Liverpool.

New Brighton's first motor-lifeboat "William & Kate Johnston" is pictured here 30 August 1924. Built at a cost of £16,084, she was 60 foot by 15 foot and was then the largest lifeboat in service with the R.N.L.I. The funds were provided by Mr. Stewart Johnston and his sister, Mrs. W. H. Kendall, of Liverpool and by the Liverpool Motor Lifeboat Fund. Officially named 24 September 1924, she was to be one of the longest serving lifeboats, operating until 1950. During that time, she was launched at least 94 times, saving 248 lives. The special net seen stretched out in the middle of the boat was an effective way of rescuing from boats higher than the lifeboat, those requiring rescue jumping into the net.

PARADE. — NEW BRIGHTON.

This photograph taken c. 1903 shows children playing on the sands wearing their Sunday best whilst promenaders stroll on the Lower Parade. This was better known as the Ham and Egg Parade. Originally built on two levels c. 1871, the higher parade, which was built on top of lock-up shops, was less exciting than the infamous lower parade which gave New Brighton a bad name. The shop proprietors would accost passers-by and entice them to view their wares or to visit their so-called tea-rooms. The council had purchased the parade properties by 1906 in order to construct the new promenade whose foundation stone was laid by William Hesketh Lever (later to become Lord Leverhulme) 22 June 1907.

The Pier Pavilion, which can be seen on the end of the pier in the previous picture, is photographed here in 1914. It dated back to at least 1892 when it was described in a local guide as a "covered saloon 130ft in length and varying in width from 28ft to 34ft — it is available for bazaars, flower-shows, concerts, balls etc." In 1899 Adeler & Sutton's Pierrots transferred from the shore to the Pier Pavilion and caused a sensation. The interior of the pavilion was completely re-constructed, re-decorated and heated throughout, re-opening March 1910. The Pier Pavilion closed in 1923 and was demolished in 1928, following the purchase by Wallasey Council (see below).

PIER AND LINER, NEW BRIGHTON.   No 3623.

"Pierrots on Parade 3.00pm & 7.30pm Daily" says the sign on the Promenade Pier in 1936. This pier was opened in September 1867, replacing the original one, for ferry access only, which dated back to the 1830's. The pier on the right was for passengers using the ferry to Liverpool and the one on the left was for amusements. The audience for the open-air pierrot show can be seen beneath the "Promenade Pier" sign and above it is the bandstand with the pavilion to the left. These two buildings were erected following the council purchasing the condemned pier in 1928. It opened following repairs in 1931. The liner to the right would be a typical sight in the 1930's.

The base of New Brighton Tower can be seen on the left in 1904, with part of its steel structure above. The Tower was opened in 1900 to attract workers from Lancashire and the Midlands here for their holidays, rather than other resorts. This is why it was built more than one hundred feet higher above sea-level than Blackpool Tower. The entrance to the thirty-five acres of ground was under the "Dancing All Day" sign on the left. The Tower was most popular prior to World War I and then, due to lack of maintenance during the war, the steel structure was demolished between 1919 and 1921. The Tower building was damaged by fire on 5 April 1969 and later demolished. The Tivoli Theatre was built on the amusement site to the right (see below).

The Tivoli Theatre to the right of the Tower (see previous picture) was opened on the Tower Promenade 6 April 1914, with Lily Langtry topping the bill. Ideally situated between the pier and the Tower, its six shops and café above did a roaring trade. The theatre, which changed hands many times, produced live shows but was also used as a cinema between 1923 and 1930. Having survived bomb damage during the war, several closures and changes of management, its theatre days came to an end in April 1955. It re-opened as the Tivoli Fair which was an indoor amusement arcade containing amusement machines, bingo, gifts, toys etc. The end came following a fire in 1976 when the Tivoli was finally demolished.

The Cummins-Brown stage-coach is seen in the picturesque parade which started at Lime Street Station in Liverpool. It wended its way down to the Pier Head, across on the ferry boat to Wirral and then to the New Brighton Tower grounds. This was to advertise a Wild West and Indian Congress which was held in the sports arena (see next picture) from 23 May to 7 October 1908. It included cowboys successfully defending their stage-coach from an Indian attack, an Indian attack on a hut which was burnt down, riding bucking horses, lasoo throwing and herding steers. Authentic steers were not allowed into the country, so wild highland cattle were acquired from Scotland and proved quite a challenge to the cowboys!

The New Brighton Tower Company's athletic arena, which was situated within the thirty-five acres of ground, was opened in 1899 and can be seen in the aerial view on page 64 in front of the Tower. The centre of the arena was used to stage many spectacular events including the Cummins-Brown show mentioned above. The inside track, pictured to the right, was used for athletics and the banked outside track was where the World Cycling Championships were held 28 July 1922. The crowds are cheering on the local hero, Mr. G. E. Tottey of Tottey's Garage, West Kirby, who held many world motorcycle records during his career. he is seen here on 5 June 1922 travelling at 50 mph.

New Brighton Railway Station exterior is pictured c. 1910 in Atherton Street at its junction with Victoria Road and only a short distance from the beach. It was opened 30 March 1888 by the Seacombe, Hoylake and Deeside Railway which merged with the Wirral Railways Company Limited in 1891 to form the Wirral Railway. That company's heraldic badge which can be seen to the left of the large "Railway Station" sign is still there today. The railway transported many residents to their work throughout the year but its busiest period was during the summer months when it carried holidaymakers and day-trippers to the resort. The large "Station" sign on the left, which could be seen from Victoria Road, guided travellers to the trains.

WINTER GARDENS THEATRE, New Brighton
MONDAY, APRIL **9th**   ::   For Six Nights at 8-0
MATINEE SATURDAY, at 3-0

PERSONAL VISIT

From a recent Photo by Dorothy Wilding

GODFREY TEARLE
WITH
MARY MALONE
AND LONDON COMPANY, IN A NEW MODERN PLAY,
"THE ACQUITTAL"
By RITA WEIMAN
(By arrangement with GEORGE M COHAN)

D. A. & S., LTD.

Further down Atherton Street on the same side as the station pictured above, stood a Conservative Hall, a single-storied building which was leased in 1907 by Albert Douglass and Mr. H. E. Jones. They renamed it Alexandra Hall, presenting shows on Saturday nights. In February 1908 the name changed to the Winter Gardens and a year later a limited company purchased the building. Alterations took place in 1910 when a balcony was erected and a new stage built with electric lighting. The next major re-building took place in 1931 when the theatre was redesigned and could show films if desired. Many London stage productions were performed here, including "The Acquittal", starring Godfrey Tearle with Mary Malone, whose advertising postcard is pictured here. In 1936, the theatre was sold to Cheshire Picture Halls Limited and in 1954 to the Essoldo Circuit. The last film was shown 3 January 1957. The building was used as a bingo hall for a few years in the mid-1960's but has remained derelict ever since.

MARINE PROMENADE, DAY NURSERY, NEW BRIGHTON.

Proud mothers with their babies and boys from the band pose for a photograph outside the Marine Park Day Nursery c. 1910. Behind the policeman on the left are the railings to Marine Park which was opened in 1897 and boasted a fine bandstand where concerts were held twice weekly. This was the westerly extent of the Marine Promenade which had been completed in 1908. It was not until 1927 that ambitious plans to extend the promenade were born (see picture below). The Nursery was demolished and after the Second World War the site was used by the police as a first-aid centre and in Spring 1974, the present Lifeboat Boathouse was opened here.

Looking up at the promenade railings from the shore in front of the Day Nursery (pictured above) whose roof can be seen behind the sand on the left. Using a wagon running on temporary rails, a gang of men are clearing sand which has drifted against a wooden sand-screen. This promenade built between 1906 and 1908 lasted until 1931 when work started on the new King's parade. The first phase, completed in 1934, went as far as the Red Noses and cost £531,000. It included a massive concrete sea wall, a promenade 130 feet wide, the marine lake, swimming baths (which now stand behind this site), and approach roads. The second phase to Harrison Drive was finished in 1939.

Frank Huck's waterplane, whose pilot, Mr. M. Fischer, is standing in the cockpit, can be seen on New Brighton beach 27 August 1912. The Daily Mail and New Brighton Pier Company had sponsored this visit by England's largest waterplane, which was assembled by two French mechanics at a local garage. Powered by Gnome Engines of 80 horsepower and eleven cylinders, this plane had one seat behind the pilot and offered flights at £2 per trip. A specially constructed raft was moored at New Brighton Pier and the plane launched from here into the water. One passenger, Miss Murry had to be rescued by boat after a gust of wind had caught the plane as it was being lowered into the water and capsized it. She was treated at the Day Nursery (see previous page) and then taken to Liscard Hospital, where she recovered. New Brighton Tower can be seen in the background, through the plane and above the crowds.

This view was one of a series of six postcards entitled "New Brighton From the Air" taken and published in 1919 by the Aircraft Manufacturing Company Limited at Hendon. Rake Lane is the main road in the centre of the picture, with Wallasey Cemetery to the left. The initial ten acre site was bought in 1880, with the first internment on 21 July 1883, and was later enlarged following further purchases. The rows of houses to the right are off Withens Lane, between Zig Zag Road and Strathcona Road. New Brighton Tower can be seen in the foreground with its top portion missing. Following lack of maintenance during the First World War period, the steel structure was demolished between May 1919 and June 1921.